WINGS LIKE
EAGLES

WINGS LIKE EAGLES

"Those who hope in the LORD will renew their strength. They will soar on wings like eagles." Isaiah 40:31

ANDREW MURRAY

CHRISTIAN ART PUBLISHERS

Published by Christian Art Publishers
PO Box 1599, Vereeniging, 1930, RSA

© 2009
First edition 2009

Cover designed by Christian Art Publishers

Image © Jason Watson, 2008
Used under license from Shutterstock.com

Scripture taken from the *Holy Bible*, New International Version®
NIV® Copyright © 1973, 1978, 1984 by International Bible Society.
Used by permission of Zondervan Publishing House. All rights reserved.

Scripture quotations are taken from the *Holy Bible*, King James Version.
Copyright © 1962 by The Zondervan Corporation. Used by permission.

Set in 11 on 14 pt New Century Schoolbook
by Christian Art Publishers

Printed in China

ISBN 978-1-77036-053-2

10 11 12 13 14 15 16 17 18 19 – 11 10 9 8 7 6 5 4 3 2

CONTENTS

PREFACE

With Wings Like Eagles passes on to its readers the words spoken by Andrew Murray at the meetings for United Prayer held in Exeter Hall on Thursday, December 5, 1895. It was a memorable day and brought to a close Andrew Murray's visit to the United Kingdom. On Saturday, December 7, Andrew Murray and his wife started on their return voyage to the Cape.

On this trip Andrew Murray spent four months in the UK, one month in America and one in Holland.

For his ministry of the Word of Christ in the United Kingdom, thousands gave thanks to God. By his established position as a writer, by his years, by his special gift from God, and by the power of the Holy Spirit, he was enabled to accomplish a service whose influence and result was long felt and remembered.

In a letter of farewell written on board ship, Andrew Murray wrote the following to the friends he left behind:

LOVE – PRAYER – GOD

My beloved brothers and sisters, may I in parting pass on these three words from our last day's meetings to you all? *Love* in the Spirit to each other, and to all saints; *prayer* in the name of Jesus; *God*, our Almighty God, to be waited on and trusted – this is a threefold cord that cannot be broken.

In the faith that our God is visiting His people, and is very near to bless them with large increase of the spirit of love and prayer, and faith in their God, I commend you to Him.

I remain,

ANDREW MURRAY

That They All
May Be One

ONE

That They All May Be One

> *"I pray ... that all of them may be one, Father,*
> *just as You are in Me and I am in You.*
> *May they also be in Us so that the*
> *world may believe that You have sent Me.*
> *I have given them the glory that*
> *You gave Me, that they may be one as*
> *We are One: I in them and You in Me.*
> *May they be brought to complete unity to let*
> *the world know that You sent Me and have*
> *loved them even as You have loved Me."*
>
> *~ John 17:20-23 ~*

The Scripture passage I wish to focus on is John 17. I will specifically deal with the following verses:

- "I pray" (v. 20).
- "That all of them may be one, Father, just as You are in Me, and I am in You. May they also be in Us so that the world may believe that You have sent Me" (v. 21).
- "I have given them the glory that You gave Me." (v. 22).

Note that the twentieth verse says, "I pray [or, I ask You]." The twenty-second verse says, "I have given them the glory that You gave Me [with the same object]: that they may be one, as We are One." The twenty-third verse says, "I in them, and You in Me. May they be brought to complete unity to let the world know that You sent Me and have loved them even as You have loved Me."

If I judge correctly what fills your heart, then I think I would express it this way: There is a deep consciousness that the overflowing love that should be among the people of God is missing. There is the desire to see this changed, and there is the secret faith: if God chooses, He is able to change us. But there is more. If we ask Him, He will pour out more love among His people.

Today we want to confess this lack of love, we want to cry to God for an increase of love.

THE ONENESS OF GOD'S PEOPLE

I don't think I need to give you examples of Christians who are failing in their love for each other. I will not speak of the divisions among the churches; I will not speak of the way in which Christians talk about each other; I will not speak of the coldness that often exists between Christians who spend years together in the same church, and eat the same bread at the Lord's Supper; I will not speak of how the most precious truths and promises of God unconsciously become walls of separation.

You all complain that there is not that expression of love that would make the world compelled to say, "God has loved them, and has poured His love into their hearts."

And now, if we are to confess, and if we are to be encouraged to pray and to hope and to expect deliverance, nothing is better than that we should turn for a few minutes to God's blessed Word – the words of our great High Priest in His last prayer. You know them well. He prayed, "Father, I pray that they may be one." It was God who was to do it. And then He added these wonderful words, "Father, between You and Me there never has been anything but love, and I want that to be among My people, that they may be one, even as We are One."

And then He says, in other words, "Father, it will be such a wonderful thing!" When selfish, proud people learn to love as the Father and the Son of God love, the world will be compelled to say, "That is more than human love; that is a love that comes from heaven."

And then Christ said, in effect, "Father, it is for this that I have given them the glory that You gave Me, and have made them partakers of the divine nature, and of all that You have. And, Father, on that account I pray for them. I have given them the glory You gave Me. And now, Father, watch over that glory, that they may be one as We are, and that they may be made perfect in one, that the world may believe that You have sent Me, and have loved them as You have loved Me." What a prayer!

Now, what are the thoughts that that prayer suggests to us about the oneness of God's people?

A Reflection of Heaven

First, the oneness among God's people is to be the reflection of the life of God in heaven. Just think of that! Heaven is the place where the glory of God is perfectly manifested; earth is the place where the reflection of that glory is to be seen. In the heavens the sun burns in all its brightness and heat and glory; here on earth, miles and miles away, is the place where its light is shining.

In heaven is the glory of God's love; but here on earth it is a beautiful, reflected light. And what is that light to be? We are to love one another and be one, just as the Father and the Son are One.

Have we really taken it in? Think of the love of the Father for the Son. What is it? The Father gave all that He had to the Son. That is His love, and that is to be my love to you and your love to me.

It is to be nothing less, for that is holiness, that is perfection, that is happiness. And God wants you holy and perfect and happy, and like Himself. That is love. God gave all He had to His beloved Son.

And what was the love of the Son for the Father? He gave all back. When He had come here to earth in the flesh, He gave all. He gave His obedience, He gave His life, He gave all to the Father. That was love. He loved the Father in eternity and sought nothing for Himself. And He loved the Father amid temptation and amid His sufferings on the earth.

That love of the Father for the Son, and that love of the Son for the Father, is to be the measure of your love to each other, children of God. I do not ask, "Have you attained that?" But I may ask, "Have you aimed at that? Has it been your study and your heart's cry: 'Oh, God, help me to love as You love, and as Jesus loves'?"

Yes, the Lord Jesus said so distinctly, and more than once, "A new command I give you: Love one another. As I have loved you, so you must love one another" (John 13:34). He came with that love, and

He was prepared by the Holy Spirit to implant it in the hearts of the disciples, who had been unloving.

"Love one another. As I have loved you, so you must love one another." Christ gave us that command. Have we understood it? It is sometimes necessary to talk about the lack of love in the church of Christ, and it is sometimes necessary to forget it, and examine my own heart instead and ask, "Am I loving my brothers and sisters in Christ?"

That is our first thought: the oneness of God's people is to be the reflection of the very life of God in heaven.

A Manifestation of God's Power

Our second thought is: That oneness of God's people is to be the manifestation of the mighty power of God. It is a thing God has to do. The Lord Jesus Christ did not say, "Father, they are one." He said, "I pray ... that they all may be one." God was to do it. Just as Christ asked God to glorify Him in heaven in the beginning of the prayer, so here at the end He asked the Father: "Do this, too, and grant that they may be one, even as We are." God Himself has to do it.

And there comes the great fault, there comes the great reason why there is so little love. We do not count on God to do it. In the heart of every child of God who is born of the Holy Spirit, God puts a seed, a principle, a power of divine love, a new will, a new heart; and every child of God is by his very nature inclined to love God's children.

But after a time there come trials, and it becomes difficult to love. And even though the Christian often tries in his own strength to love, he fails. Afterwards he gives way to despair, and he begins to do his very best to love with his little love – but he never can love as the Bible wants him to love.

He misunderstood God's plan. God's plan is, "It is God who works in you to will and to act according to His good purpose" (Phil. 2:13). When He has first worked to *will*, you are still helpless, but He wants you to come and claim the power of the Holy Spirit to enable you to *act*.

I have focused much on the Holy Spirit, but I am coming to the conviction, which grows deeper every day, that we know very little of what the Holy Spirit can do. I believe that the word of Paul, "God has poured out His love into our hearts by the Holy Spirit" (Rom. 5:5) means that just as Paul was filled with the love of God, and as Paul could say, "Christ's love compels us" (2 Cor. 5:14) and as Paul lived incessantly, day and night, praying for God's people, and as Paul poured out his love with all the tenderness of a mother as he tells us himself, so God's Holy Spirit can so fill the heart and life that love will be to us as natural as the love of a mother towards her child.

The Lord Jesus Christ, our High Priest, cried to His Father to do the work, to make us one. And we try in our own strength to love, and fail, instead of coming, utterly impotent and helpless, to claim a new blessing, to ask the Holy Spirit to fill us and shed abroad through our whole being the almighty love of God.

It is good that we long to hear about love. But everything will be like "the morning mist and the early dew" (Hosea 13:3). Our aim and purpose to love will vanish unless God gives His Holy Spirit power in our hearts.

Let every heart bow before God. We must undertake to do the work of love, and give ourselves up to intercession, and think of what God wants us to do in intercession.

If we are really to have the spirit of intercession, we must have the love of Immanuel, the Lamb of God. Ask God today to give you His love – in a measure and in a way and in a power you have never understood before. God can make your heart a vessel for that love, and He will delight in doing it.

An Answer to Prayer

Then comes my next thought, which is: Love comes in answer to prayer. I have spoken about the great power of God doing it, but I now want to point out that Christ prayed for it.

He prayed, "That they all may be one." Oh, that our hearts might just for a moment look up to see our Lord Jesus and hear by the Holy Spirit that prayer which goes up, not in words, but in His holy presence and power, "Father ... that they all may be one." He prays for them without ceasing, He lives to pray for them.

And what does that call us to do? To pray with Him in His name, in His Spirit, and with great faith in the fellowship of His intercession. When we pray for an outpouring of love in our hearts and the hearts of God's children around us, a change in the church will come.

Allow me to reveal what has been on my heart, and is on my heart – that God's children ought to pray for all believers every day of their lives. Paul did not tell Christians in his epistles to pray for the heathen, or for the Jews, or for the unconverted, but he always told them to pray for "all the saints." They are the members of your body, they are your brothers and sisters. And until we cry to God every day in our devotions for His body, the church, just as much as we cry to Him for our own souls, I do not believe that a great revival of love will come.

But I think God will pour it into the hearts of His children as the beginning, as the earnest of what He is going to do. Pray for Christians every day of your lives. I do not want you to give up any union that you may have joined, to pray at certain times for certain circles or for all believers, but I want you to feel that it ought to be a continuous part of your spiritual life.

Just as close as my relation to Christ is my relation to my fellow Christians; as dependent as I am upon Christ in some things, I am dependent on others for the fellowship of believers. Every thought of Christ ought to be linked with the thought of His people, His body, the church. By prayer it will come.

May God give us the very spirit of prayer to call upon Him. But may God give the spirit of prayer in our hearts in such a way that a cry shall come from us continually, "God, make us one, as You and Your Son are One." The cry will lead us to feel our own helplessness and the loneliness and feebleness of our lives.

Remember that Paul said in 1 Thessalonians 4:9-10, "You yourselves have been taught by God to love each other. And in fact, you do love all the brothers throughout Macedonia." And yet he wrote calling upon them, "Do so more and more." There is an increase of love when the Holy Spirit touches the heart. Then the love will flow in a stream, and it will be one of those streams of which Jesus spoke when He said, "Whoever believes in Me, streams of living water will flow from within him" (John 7:38).

Those living waters are to impart what the

fountain has got, and thereby make everything around them green and fresh: the stream of love will impart of itself to bless others. We must pray that this oneness may be made manifest.

Proof of God's Love

The manifestation of the oneness between God's people on earth is to be proof to the world that God sent Christ and that God has loved us. Just think of that. How important it is! You know Christ Jesus Himself said, "By this all men will know that you are My disciples [a heavenly people], if you love one another" (John 13:35). That is to be the heavenly hallmark, and Jesus says it twice in our text.

First of all, He says, "I pray that all of them may be one, so that the world may believe that You have sent Me." You know that Christ was among them in the world, and they would not believe it. And what was to bring conviction? Love. That is what Christ said. Not preaching, but *love*. Preaching is needed – praise God for what it does! – but love will do more.

Then Jesus says, "I have given them the glory that You gave Me, that they may be one as We are One. May they be brought to complete unity to let the world know that You sent Me and have loved them even as You have loved Me."

God loved Christ with a wonderful love, and

God loves His people with that same love; and the love with which God loves Christ became a love that He poured out upon us even unto the blood of Calvary. The love with which God and Christ love us is a power within us that will pour itself out, in the first place, for believers; and thereby the world will be convinced.

People speak of the evidences of Christianity, and books have been written on the evidences of Christianity, and they are not without their value, though I do not know that they have turned many from darkness to light. But Christ says it is love that will compel the world to say; "These people have got something from heaven. These people are living a superhuman life. Look at the way in which they love each other!"

Has the world around you, or any part of it, been convinced, convicted, and brought to acknowledge, "God sent Christ, and God loved you just as He loved Christ. I can see it, for there is something in you that I do not find upon earth"? If so, then praise God!

There have been such cases. There are believers of whom others have felt that they have something that is not of the earth. But how little this happens! And yet it should be the case with each one of us! Just one thing is needed in order to show the world that we are different: We must wait upon God in prayer.

Let me point out to you one verse to impress this thought upon you. First Thessalonians 3:12 says, "May the Lord make your love increase and overflow for each other and for everyone else."

Now note that just as Christ prayed to the Father, so Paul prayed, "The Lord make your love increase and overflow." And he uses the same expression in the ninth and tenth verses of the fourth chapter; "About brotherly love we do not need to write to you, for you yourselves have been taught by God to love each other. And in fact, you do love all the brothers throughout Macedonia. Yet we urge you, brothers, to do so more and more."

Christ said in effect, "Love one another, as I have loved you." And Paul said the same, "The Lord make your love increase and overflow for each other."

And now I urge you to notice the words which follow in 1 Thessalonians 3:13, "May He strengthen your hearts so that you will be blameless and holy in the presence of our God."

How is God going to make me holy and establish my heart blameless in holiness? By filling me with love. Love is the fulfilling of the whole law, and the perfection of the life of God and of Christ. And when God makes us to increase and abound in love toward one another, then self sinks away and the love of God takes possession. When this happens, the love and the holiness of God can grow and prosper and rule within us.

Let us take that prayer today, "The Lord make us to increase and abound in love toward one another, so that He may establish our hearts as blameless and holy in His sight."

The Heart of Love

So what is needed if this love of God is to come and take possession of our souls? The heart must be utterly and absolutely given up to God to love. May God enable us to see how little there has been of the real heavenly love within us! May God enable us to confess and repent of it!

How much self has limited our love to people that we agree with, and to people that we like, and to people who think just as we do! How much our love has been limited within our own circle, and how little it has gone out, like the love of Christ, to the unworthy, to those who differ from us, to those who do not love us!

Have you earnestly tried to love every person whom you would rather be separate from? Have you made it a study to pray, "Lord, here is one in whom my love can triumph, in whom Your love can triumph; I want to love him as a brother"? May God give us the spirit of humility to be able to confess how little divine love we actually have.

Every now and then, when we fail, we see that the spirit of love has not yet triumphed within us.

But praise God the Father on whom Christ called, to whom Paul prayed, to whom we come to pray today – the Father in heaven who wants to give His Holy Spirit of love to us.

Even before we make intercession for an outpouring of the Spirit of love upon the church, we must begin by asking for an outpouring of the Spirit into our own hearts. We should say, "Lord God, empty our hearts of self, we desire to confess and give up everything that is selfish; we desire to study and aim at this one thing – to live on earth towards every brother as God and Christ live together in heaven."

You might say, "But God and Christ see in Each Other nothing but what is lovely. How can They do otherwise than love Each Other? But my brother tempts me so! There is so much in him that is hard and unlovable!" Yet that is why the Son of God came to earth, to prove that the love of God in heaven could stand the trials of life – every enmity, every shame, every suffering – and live through it all.

It is your high privilege to have your heart filled with the heavenly love of Christ Jesus, and to carry it through life; and it is your high privilege to begin and prove that you love your brother. You might find it difficult to love the ungodly, and yet sometimes you say, "I find it easier to love the ungodly than to love my very brother." This is wrong! Praise God that you can love the ungodly through His Spirit.

If you can do that, how then can you not love your brother – someone who is redeemed with the blood of Christ, and made a member of one body in one Spirit with you through Christ!

Let us confess our sin, our utter helplessness, and then let us look up in faith and claim the mighty power of God's Spirit. Let us claim in faith the promise in Romans 5:5, "God has poured out His love into our hearts by the Holy Spirit, whom He has given us."

Then, when we have truly yielded ourselves to God, let us begin to plead and pray for God's church around us, for every child of God. Let us begin to pray a prayer that shall never cease, "Lord, visit your believers." Oh, that God may write this upon our hearts!

Are you willing to give yourself up to this glorious work of praying believers and for a revelation of God's love in Christ's body? Let your heart say to God, "Lord, here am I." Then you will receive a blessing of love.

If you want love for yourself, or love that is going to plead for the body of Christ, then you must do two things. Go and confess your lack of love to God, and then say, "Lord God, I want to have that love, that from this day on I may pray daily for Your Church, for all believers." God will give you what you ask for; the great intercession of Christ secures it.

The key to being united as believers

and as a church is to love one

another with the love of God.

The Secret of
Effectual Prayer

TWO

The Secret of Effectual Prayer

In the same way, the Spirit helps us in our weakness. We do not know what we ought to pray for, but the Spirit Himself intercedes for us with groans that words cannot express. And He who searches our hearts knows the mind of the Spirit, because the Spirit intercedes for the saints in accordance with God's will.

~ Romans 8:26-27 ~

In these words we find the secret of effectual prayer. I have had someone complain to me, "I feel so little love for prayer and power for prayer!" The power for prayer is the Holy Spirit. So many complain that they do not feel strong stirrings of desire in intercession for others, but there is a secret power: "the Spirit helps us in our weakness." May we learn that precious lesson!

ACKNOWLEDGE YOUR IGNORANCE IN PRAYER

What are the thoughts suggested to us here? The first thought is this: If you want to discover the secret of effectual prayer, you must begin with a sense of your own ignorance. When someone says, "I can pray," there is no room for the Spirit to work in full power. It is only when a person says, "I cannot pray," that the Holy Spirit comes.

And how often we think it is easy to pray. We think, "I learned it from my mother; I learned it from my minister; I learned it when I was converted; I learned it from written prayers." And so, although we think we know *how* to pray, we may not know what God wants us to pray *for*. We may be praying very earnestly for what we think, but we are not allowing God's Spirit to teach us what God thinks.

Therefore, if you want to pray in power begin

with these words, "The Spirit helps us in our weakness." Just as Paul said, "When am I weak, then am I strong ... that Christ's power may rest on me" (2 Cor. 12:10, 9).

So it is when I feel my weakness in prayer that the Holy Spirit will help me. It is when I learn to say, and not only to say, but when I live in the experience and consciousness of, "I know not what I ought to pray for," that I have a claim upon the promise of the Holy Spirit's help.

Have you ever studied the blessedness of ignorance? Oh, the divine blessedness of ignorance! "God chose the foolish things of the world" (1 Cor. 1:27). That is not just an idea – it is a reality. Abraham went out not knowing where he was going, but he had God as his Guide. So through the whole of God's Word you will find that when a man is ignorant and at his wits' end and says, "I don't know what to do," God comes in and takes charge.

Remember, the Holy Spirit cannot come to you in prayer as the Spirit of prayer and intercession unless this double thought is deep in your life, "I do not know what I ought to pray for, and I do not know how to pray."

There are so many Christians who think that thought is a terrible burden and a great sorrow. But I tell you it is your highest privilege, if you use it correctly and say, "Lord, I cannot pray, but let Your blessed Spirit pray with me."

In the great work of intercession that we will engage in and undertake, let us remember that our ignorance will be the secret of success if we use it correctly.

"I know what to pray for," you say. "Yes, I can read my Bible. I know the needs of my heart. I know the needs of the world around me. Oh yes, I need to pray for my country, and for God's church, and for the unsaved." But so much of that praying is the work of the mind, the work of the flesh, the work of man!

Do not be afraid to identify with the words, "We know not what to pray for as we ought." That is the first step.

ACKNOWLEDGE THE HOLY SPIRIT AS A PRAYER TEACHER

What is next? That we begin to learn that the Holy Spirit has been given from heaven into our hearts to teach us to pray. "The Spirit helps us in our weakness." Have you realized that God not only answers prayer, but that, dwelling within us by the Holy Spirit, He inspires prayer? If that is true, what would be the effect of my believing fully?

It would be, first of all, a lowering of yourself before God, a humiliation and a dependence expressed as, "Oh, God, may I not, in my flesh, or in my thoughts hinder Your blessed Spirit." And then there would come a deep subjection and surrender to the Spirit, and the deep consciousness that says, "I must give up my life for Him to live in me, or He cannot pray in me."

We must not think that we can just get the Holy Spirit to come and do something for us. We should understand that God must be the very Spirit of our lives, and He must have entire possession of us.

Have you ever learned this solemn, blessed lesson: the Holy Spirit and I are linked together in prayer? And God desires that the Holy Spirit, dwelling in the body of Christ, should teach each individual person of that body to pray aligned in the power of faith. Have you ever learned that lesson? If not, pray that God will open it up and reveal it to you.

And when the question comes, "What is needed for me to get the teaching of the Spirit?" the answer will be this, "As a surrendered soul, I am entirely at His disposal. He is not an entity outside of me. He comes in to be my very life. Unless I give myself up to Him, how can He do His blessed work and fully teach me how to pray?"

That brings us to a very solemn point. Some days ago, someone was telling me of another person that she wanted to bring with her to the meetings and she said, "I am afraid she is not a surrendered soul." In another case somebody said of one who was going to come, "He is still undecided – half-way between Christ and the world!"

Now, if there are souls here, children of God, who are not utterly surrendered to Him, I plead with you, before I go further, to think about it. The Holy Spirit cannot dwell in a worldly heart; the Holy Spirit cannot do His blessed work in a life that is not given up to Him. Come today, if you have any desire for a full blessing, and say, "If God has given His Holy Spirit to pray in me, I will give my whole heart to Him."

If you have never yet in faith claimed the promise of the full indwelling of the Holy Spirit, come today and claim it. Your God offers you the Holy Spirit to pray in you, and how can He do it if you don't follow Him, if you distrust Him, and if you dishonor Him with unbelief? I want to invite all God's children here to become intercessors. But we cannot do it unless we all join and say, "God, reveal to us everything in which the Holy Spirit does not have complete possession. We desire to give it up, and to be filled with Your Spirit."

I feel more and more deeply, every time I address meetings, that there may be an earnest Christian, a godly man or woman, and yet his or her life is far below what God could make it, if he or she would only wait for the Holy Spirit to rule in their hearts.

I want to call you to be intercessors. I want to

plead with you by the needs of this city with its millions of people, by the needs of the hundreds of millions of unsaved people, and by the needs of the church of Christ, with its multitudes of people who just profess to follow God, and half-hearted Christians, will you not be intercessors? Will you not give up yourselves to walk in the footsteps of Christ and become fountains of blessing to this weary world?

Let the Holy Spirit have you entirely today, and then He will teach you how to pray.

Acknowledge the Way in Which the Holy Spirit Prays

A third thought is this: We must understand the way in which the Holy Spirit will pray. And how is that? "The Spirit helps us in our weakness. We do not know what we ought to pray for, but the Spirit Himself intercedes for us with groans that words cannot express." What is that? Prayers too deep for words! That is what we want.

When words rise into prayer so fluently and so easily, the depth of the heart is often not stirred. But what is it that the Holy Spirit wants to do? How often we see it in our blessed Lord Jesus! He once said, "I have a baptism to undergo, and how distressed I am until it is completed!" (Luke 12:50). Remember that He said, "And what shall I say?

'Father, save Me from this hour'?" (John 12:27). He did not know at the moment what He should say.

Remember how in Gethsemane He wrestled and wrestled with His emotions, and yet had but few words with which to utter the agony of His heart?

When the Holy Spirit fills us as the fire of God's love for souls, and we begin to think of the state of Christ's body, of fellow believers in the church of Christ, of our own lack of love and tenderness and gentleness, of the feebleness that marks God's people, of the way the world loves to scorn our puny efforts, and of the millions that are succumbing to misery – surely we will feel, if God's Spirit lives in us, compassion, an intensity and desire too deep for words! That is the time when the Holy Spirit prays in us "with groans that words cannot express."

We read of creation "groaning." There is a moan throughout the whole of creation, and a longing for redemption. The animals do not speak it out in words, but throughout creation there is a groan. Even so, the deeper God's child is led into the fellowship of Christ and love for others, the deeper and the truer his sympathy is for the perishing.

There will come times when all he can do is sit still before God, and say, "Lord, what is going to happen? Teach me what I may ask, teach me what I may pray." And while he feels, "I cannot pray," God has heard in that heart a better prayer than one that flows smoothly and quickly from the lips.

Many people think that when they have been in their closet and prayer has flowed easily, that they have prayed well. At other times, when prayer has not flowed easily, they think that they have not prayed well. And yet, if that silent prayer is mingled with true faith, a waiting upon God, and a deep burning desire, it is sweeter incense to the Father than a prayer full of flowing words.

Oh, it is a solemn thing for the worm of the dust to get linked to the Holy Spirit of God. You need not wonder if the Holy Spirit of God will sometimes come with wrestlings and groanings which cannot be uttered; but the privilege and blessedness of this act are unspeakable. Yield yourself to Him.

BELIEVE THAT THE ANSWER WILL COME

The last thought in my text is this: The believer must know how the answer will come. How can it come when you sit there saddened and bowed down with a burden you cannot speak of?

Listen! "He who searches our hearts knows the mind of the Spirit, because the Spirit intercedes for the saints in accordance with God's will." God, the heart-searcher, is needed to find out the meaning of prayer.

You may think you know it, but you do not. It needs God in heaven, who searches our hearts, to measure the real value of our prayers. We deceive ourselves.

We have sometimes thought, "Oh, that man can pray!" And we believed him to be a Christian, but have been disappointed afterwards because his life was not like his prayer. We have sometimes heard ourselves pray, thought that God helped, and yet afterwards we felt that that prayer showed only half the life. There was another half. But the Searcher of hearts never makes a mistake; the Searcher of hearts searches the divine life of every breath of the Spirit.

Child of God, give yourself up to the Holy Spirit to pray even when you feel you have nothing much to say. He who searches the heart knows what the mind of the Spirit is. And why? It says, "The Spirit intercedes for the saints." Note the words "for the saints." Earlier I quoted the words of Paul, "Keep on praying for all the saints" (Eph. 6:18).

Some think that the word does not only refer to those who are praying, but that it also has a wider meaning; that it is the Holy Spirit's one work to make supplication for all believers.

Therefore, if you want this power of the Holy Spirit to pray, you must not confine Him to yourself or you will lose a great deal. Take Him for what He is given for – to make supplication and intercession for all believers. Unite yourself to Him, and let Him unite Himself to you, and give up yourself to make intercession for all believers.

The Holy Spirit prays within us, and God searches our hearts. There is nothing that God finds more delight in than to find love in and for all of His children. I urge you to make a study of that.

Suppose you know a legalist. The inclination is to condemn him. You stand at the opposite moral pole and think about how he may be destroying some people's religious lives. Pray for him!

You may hear a man – a child of God – speak and you don't agree with his doctrine and you have a sharp word about him. But I ask you instead to pray for him.

If there is someone in your circle of friends who has hurt you, love and pray for him. Make intercession.

Need I remind you that the thought of intercession is a very wonderful one? Christ sits as King upon the throne. Yes, and what is the work of a king? To rule, to have honor and power and glory and dominion. And Christ has that. But even with all that, upon His kingly throne He ever lives to pray.

If an earthly king spent all his free time praying for his subjects, imagine how people would talk about his piety and godliness! Our King's great work is to pray, and His great desire in sending down the Holy Spirit into our hearts is that we should pray with Him.

How much of your life have you given up to intercession? Or how little? God knows. There is not one among us who doesn't have reason to blush at that fact. But God forgives! And He works a change by His almighty grace and He strengthens every one who is trying to learn to pray.

Someone once expressed a hope that this meeting would be "a day with Christ in the school of prayer." God, grant it! Oh, that our great Intercessor and High Priest might condescend to breathe upon us, to touch us, to draw us, to link us with Himself in prayer. But He can only do it if our hearts are given up to the Holy Spirit.

ANOINTED BY THE SPIRIT

Let me conclude by pointing out what the work is that we have to do. We want to intercede for our city very definitely. May God bless every prayer circle that binds His children together to cry to Him. But we need something more. If only all God's children could learn, "I am anointed of the Holy Spirit, the Spirit of intercession, that I may do my work!"

What is the reason for the feeble Christianity prevalent in the world? Why are there so many souls complaining about their lack of power and joy? It is this – the selfishness of our religion. We have come to Christ to be saved, and that is the main thing. And then a little intercession and a little work we do alongside with the rest.

But we must come round to an entirely different position and perspective. We must say, "I have been redeemed to be a member of Christ's body, and, like Christ, to live holy and be a blessing to the world, and to communicate God's love to others."

But you cannot do that without giving up yourselves entirely to Him. Praise God for every child of His whose eyes have been opened to see it, and whose heart has been stirred to make the blessed choice, "Yes, Lord, everything, every breath, that Your name may be exalted!" Praise God for every child of His whose heart recognizes, "I have not been living like this, but I am going to live it from today." God help us!

I cannot press upon you the importance of praying for all believers. I charge you to take it up as your life's work to bring the Christian church before God in heaven. Live to pray. You pray for your work, and for your family and friends, and for many interests, and I praise God for it. Pray for these, and not less.

But pray first and foremost, in the power of the Spirit of intercession, for all believers. Pray for every believer in the world. If you do this, your heart will fill up with love.

Pray for every believer who has strayed from God's path. You cannot pray for a person for long without beginning to love him and to be humbled before the Lord. May God pour out His Spirit. May He teach us what it means to have the Holy Spirit work in our hearts as the Spirit of intercession!

I'm sure you have heard more than one address and appeal from time to time over the years about the baptism of the Holy Spirit. You have heard appeals about being filled with the Spirit, about being led by the Spirit, about walking in the Spirit. But remember, the Spirit is the Spirit of intercession for all believers. You cannot have Him to yourself. He is the Spirit of the body.

Today let us do two things. Firstly, let us give up ourselves to the Holy Spirit as the Spirit of intercession to pray in us, and declare that we desire to live for God, and for His church.

Secondly, in our prayers and in our lives, let this thought be our constant source of joy and strength, "However ignorant I feel, and however feeble my words may be, the Spirit prays in me, and God who searches the hearts knows the mind of the Spirit."

Live to pray. Pray with the help of

the Holy Spirit and your prayers

will be effectual and powerful.

With Eagles' Wings

THREE

With Eagles' Wings

---

*Those who hope in the LORD will renew
their strength. They will soar on wings like eagles;
they will run and not grow weary,
they will walk and not be faint.*

~ Isaiah 40:31 ~

The theme of this message could be titled *Working and Waiting*. All that we have been asking God to do must manifest itself in new work, more work, and better work.

Those who have never worked cannot earnestly ask God to honor them with the indwelling of His heavenly love, if they are going to continue to live selfish lives.

They cannot sincerely pray, "Oh, God, let Your own blessed love fill me, and then I will spend it. I will give it out. I will scatter the blessing."

And those who have been working, oh, how conscious they are of the feebleness of their work! It is not always more work that is needed – some might even be able to work less. The important thing is the quality of work that is done.

We pray to God for His mercy to be upon our city, and upon the workers in our city, and for grace that every one of us might go out to live in the power of God's strength and love. It is hardly necessary that I should speak in-depth about the secret of strength for work. That is what we all need.

As God's children, we are promised a divine strength that is already prepared for us. But many of us are unaware of it or do not know how to receive it. And just as that one word *work* means so much, earthward and manward, so the word *wait* means everything Godward. And your work towards people, if it is to bring blessing, will depend entirely upon your waiting upon God.

Read the words of the verse again, "Those who hope in the LORD will renew their strength." Every day, "they will run" and never "grow weary, they will walk and not be faint."

Blessed life! To work, work, work, though your body and mind are weary, in times of despair and failure, and yet to never be weary in spirit, but to carry on with the joy of God! What a kind Master!

You can see in His servants that He cares for them. His servants are children and heirs of God, and will God allow them to be weary in spirit? Never, if they will come and dwell with Him as He is ready to have them. Those who hope in the LORD will renew their strength, and will always be strong for work.

How I wish I had known that when I was a young minister! How I wish I knew it fully even now! I thank God for what He has shown me of it but pray that He might reveal it even more fully to my soul and to every soul here that those who wait upon the Lord in hope, will always have new strength; "they will run and not grow weary, they will walk and not be faint."

How many are faint-hearted in their work, and stop working, or work wearily, or work very little, or work with effort and struggle? And all because they do not know the joy of the Lord! May God teach us how to work.

SOARING ON EAGLES' WINGS

"Those who hope in the LORD will renew their strength. They will soar on wings like eagles." Let me take that one expression first. Most of you have heard sermons preached on this verse, I am sure. But just let me give you two or three very simple thoughts about soaring on eagles' wings.

The eagle is called the king of birds. It is said to fly the highest heights of all the birds, and to fly straight toward the sun. And this king of birds is taken to be the image of God's children. Why? What are eagles' wings for? To carry the king of birds high up into heaven.

You are a heavenly creature, and you are to lead a heavenly life. Your place is in the heavenlies. And how can you rise to heaven unless you have wings like eagles to soar on? If God created the eagles with their wings to rise high heavenward, He can give you wings, so that you too can rise upward.

Yes, the believer is to live a heavenly life. His home is within the veil, in the holiest of all. He is to walk on "high places." He is to live in the love of God, with the joy of heaven in his heart. He is to live a life in which the will of God is done, as in heaven so on earth. The Christian needs eagles' wings.

Unfortunately many Christians are bound and

weighed down! Once when I was in Switzerland I saw an eagle, a splendid bird, but it was chained to a rock. It had about twenty or thirty feet of chain attached to its legs, which was fastened to an iron bolt in the rock. There was the king of birds, made to soar into heaven, chained down to earth.

This is a picture of many believers. Is it your life? Are you just plodding along through life? You are a child of God! That eagle was a king of birds, a noble king, but something kept it down. Are you allowing the cares of the world, business worries, or your flesh, to chain you down so that you cannot rise up?

This should not be so. I invite every believer to say, "God help me to soar on eagles' wings; I want to live the heavenly life." God help us!

And then you ask, "How can I get these wings?" I answer, "How did the eagle get its wings? By its birth. It was born a royal eagle; it had a royal descent."

Every child of God is born with wings like eagles. But unfortunately they don't know it. We are all born with wings, we have within us a divine nature; the very Spirit of Christ Jesus to draw us heavenward.

So many believers do not know that they have the Spirit of heaven within them. Even those who just barely know it, do not think of it, accept it, or rejoice in it! So many believers have got a little inkling of it, but are unfaithful, and turn themselves away toward the world – again! I tell you, you have a divine nature, you have a heavenly nature; God means you to live a heavenly life!

You tell me, "If I have these eagle wings that I have never used, how can I learn to use them?"

I will give you the answer. You may have heard it before, but listen once again. In Deuteronomy, Moses tells us about God, how, just as the eagle soars up to its nest and flutters over its young and carries them on its back, so God carried Israel. What does that mean?

Look at the distant cliffs by the sea, some thousand feet high, and up on a ledge of rock there is an eagle's nest, and the little birds have just been born. Come another day, and what do you see? The nest is nothing but a number of sticks gathered together and laid across, and there are the little eaglets. The mother eagle comes, stirs up her nest with her beak and claw, and scatters it.

And then what does she do? The little eaglets have looked over the cliff, and they have seen the deep sea down below, and they are afraid. The mother, however, casts them over the edge, and then they go fluttering about, threatening to fall and drown.

But see how the mother hangs over them, and goes in under them, and stretches her broad wings, and catches first the one and then the other, and carries them on her back to some place of safety. God made the eagle with that instinct, and that is a picture of God's own heart too.

How does God teach His eaglet children to use their wings? He comes and stirs up their nests. How does He do that? Sometimes with a trying situation, death, sickness, loss, tribulation or temptation.

And why? Just as those eaglets, ready to fall, find their mother coming under them and carrying them, so the everlasting arms are stretched out underneath the soul that feels itself about to perish, and God calls upon the soul to trust Him.

As the eaglet trusts the mother to carry it, so God asks you to trust Him, trust Him to carry you. The mother bears the little eaglet time after time, and later the eaglet begins to take courage, and at last is ready to soar forth, for it has learned to use its wings. The mother taught it. And my God longs to teach His children also to soar on eagle wings.

But how can they do it? It says, "Those who hope in the LORD will soar on wings like eagles." Yes, God often comes to the Christian worker and stirs up the nest because He sees the eagle wings are not being used.

God might find a worker to be very earnest, and perhaps for a time there has been blessing, but somehow self-will and the power of the flesh have come in. He has begun to trust only in himself, so

God comes and stirs up his nest. Then the Christian worker asks, "What is this? Have I served my God as I should have done, or have I sinned against Him?"

Then God's blessed Word comes with a message to this effect, "No, your Father loves you, but there is one thing He misses about you – you are not heavenly enough. You have worked hard, and you have worked well, and you have worked successfully; but the tenderness and the beauty of the heavenly love of Jesus are too little seen in you. The Father wants you to soar on eagle wings. Your fellowship with God is not as tender as it ought to be, so God has stirred up and broken your nest."

Then the worker becomes anxious, and fears that everything will perish. The power he thought he had fails him.

We need to learn to see that God wants us to trust Him more, He wants us to come into a closer union with Himself.

The King James Version of the same verse says, "They that *wait* upon the LORD shall renew their strength." They shall go on from strength to strength, they shall get stronger month by month, and year by year. They shall renew their strength, and they will soar on eagle wings.

God, help us to believe it and to say, "That is going to be my lot, a life of mounting up on eagle wings." Do you dare to say that? Yes, you dare say it, if you dare say, "My life shall be one of waiting upon God."

RENEWED STRENGTH

What are the characteristics of an eagle's wings? To be able to soar to heaven, the wings of the eagle must have greater strength than the wings of any other bird. And God wants His children to be so strong that they can live above the world and can show the men of the world, "I am living in another world."

The great mark of the disciple of Christ that Christ spoke of in His prayer to the Father was, "They are not of the world, even as I am not of it" (John 17:16). They belong to heaven, their life and heart are there. It is up to you to believe that in your business in this city, in a house full of worry and anxiety, you can live a heavenly life in the peace, love and joy of God.

Eagles' wings are strong; they can resist the gravitation and the attraction of earth, they can rise heavenward. Praise God, we can live heavenly lives!

This idea is the foundation of our text. Look at the words that precede it in Isaiah 40:28-29, "Do you not know? Have you not heard? The LORD is the everlasting God, the Creator of the ends of the earth. He will not grow tired or weary, and His understanding no one can fathom."

Let me ask you, weary worker, have you heard it, do you know it, that the everlasting God is never weary? You say, "Of course, I have known it all my life, and I have believed it." Then believe it in the appeal God makes.

You ask, "What is that appeal?" The appeal is that if the everlasting God is never weary, you need never be weary either, because your God is your strength. That is what the Bible teaches. You have no strength but what God gives, and God makes all strength available to us.

Have you heard it, weary worker? Have you heard it, you who fears you can work but little? Have you heard it, earnest intercessor, who fears that the blessing will not come as you would have it? Listen! "Have you not heard? The LORD is the everlasting God, the Creator of the ends of the earth. He will not grow tired or weary." Think about that!

You find that word *weary* four times in the passage. First, it is God who does not grow *weary* (v. 28); then it is, He gives strength to the *weary* (v. 29); and then the youths grow *weary* (v. 30). (All human strength shall *weary*; the very strongest shall grow *weary* and be of no avail.) And last, "They will run and not grow *weary*" (v. 31).

I pray that you understand this wonderful teaching. There is the Everlasting and Almighty One, and you are asked to look at Him with His mighty creative power, and His power in trouble.

This evening I read the verse, "Lift your eyes and look to the heavens: Who created all these? He who brings out the starry host one by one, and calls them each by name. Because of His great power and mighty strength, not one of them is missing" (Isa. 40:26).

Every star was made to show you that God cares for them all, and God's power upholds them. And God's power upholds you much more, child of God. May we begin to believe in the power of Almighty God! I pray to God that I believe in it fully; my heart longs to do so.

I believe that if there is one lesson we need to learn; it is the lesson of our helplessness. When I was studying and learning to be a Christian as a young man, I was told a great deal about my lack of righteousness, and about my want of goodness, and about my absolute worthlessness. I believed it, and I believe it still. In myself I have no righteousness before God. But I was never taught correctly. (At least I was not taught it so clearly as that it entered my heart. It may have been my fault, but since that time I have found so many who have not been taught it.)

I was never taught that just as little righteousness as you have, just as little strength as you have, and just as much as you are dependent on the righteousness of Christ alone for salvation, this is how dependent you are on the strength of God alone for sanctification.

I was not taught that, and that is the truth of God that if you are to live a holy life and work for God, you must learn, "My only hope of being holy and working correctly is the everlasting God in heaven." Then follows the promise, "He gives strength to the weary and increases the power of the weak."

God offers Himself to be the power and the strength and the might of every one of His children. Isn't that what we need in all our religious work – to get to that secret place of God's power, where the power of God can work in us?

WAITING ON THE LORD

You ask, and you cannot ask a more important question, "How can I get that power?" This is the glorious answer, "They that wait upon the LORD shall renew their strength" (KJV). Where do I find the power to use eagle wings to mount and soar and rise higher and higher? In waiting upon God.

There are people who cannot understand this idea of waiting on God. One beloved brother in the ministry asked me last week, "Is there not a danger of becoming too passive?"

I said, "Oh, yes, my brother, as long as we think it is our activity that must do it, then passivity robs us of time and strength. But once we understand that it is God who must work it in us, then we begin to understand that our highest passivity will be our highest activity, for when we give ourselves entirely away to God, God can work in us. Then we shall work as people who "wait upon the Lord."

Let us now for a few minutes try and think what waiting on the Lord means. I want to give it to you as my parting word.

When I last came to Exeter Hall, we had a breakfast, attended by approximately one hundred and twenty friends. I spoke on that occasion and gave one of the simplest messages that there could be to point out that waiting upon God is the one thing the church needs. I have been perfectly surprised to find what a response that simple word has created in the hearts of God's children. And so I give you that word tonight: "They that wait upon the Lord shall renew their strength" (KJV).

What is needed to live such a life? My answer is, first of all, if you are to wait upon the Lord, you must learn to know Him. You must turn away your thoughts, eyes, heart and trust from everything, and set them on God alone. My conduct in waiting for a man, or waiting on him, will depend entirely on what I think of him.

One who waits upon the Queen will behave in a different way from one who waits upon an ordinary person. All our waiting upon God will depend upon one thing – the knowledge that we have of Him.

But how does God reveal Himself when He calls us to wait upon Him? You have heard the words that I have read to show Him to be the Almighty Creator, and they tell us that just as His omnipotence created the world and is a guarantee for its maintenance, so the omnipotence of God is a guarantee for the strength of our Christian lives.

Take time to take this in. The Almighty God is with you to work in your heart all that He wants you to have. Is that true? Is God's omnipotence ready to work in you all that He expects of you? There is not a doubt about it, because you alone cannot work it. And He does not ask it of you except as He offers to work it.

Let me look at the omnipotence of God, and then at His faithfulness. He never is weary. He has kept the world going all these ages. And my short life of sixty, seventy, or eighty years – will my God not care for and maintain that? When I look at what He does for the stars, I realize that His work is being done every moment. If He withdrew His hand for one moment, the stars would fall. And God, in His omnipotence and faithfulness, is willing to work in your heart every moment of the day:

Moment by moment
I'm kept in His love,
Moment by moment

I've life from above,
Looking to Jesus
'till glory doth shine,
Moment by moment,
Oh, Lord, I am Thine.

Do I keep my property, say my watch, moment by moment? Do you think that your God will not keep you every moment? He will, if you let Him. You are invited by Him to come, and day by day to make it the chief exercise of your religious life to wait upon what your God is going to do for you, to expect it of Him, to look to Him in confidence, and in the blessed assurance that He will do it all.

Are you an earnest Christian whose life is not yet in the bright light of God's countenance? Let me speak a single word again to you about the blessedness of living in Christ moment by moment.

A young lady wrote me a letter last week, and I will tell you the story she told me in her letter. At the meetings in Whitechapel, on the evening when we spoke about absolute surrender, she wrote to me how word by word she approved, and understood, and accepted, until it came to the last, when the question was asked, "Will you now absolutely surrender?" Then her fears got the better of her, and she went away very miserable.

She came again the next morning and afternoon and evening, and then we spoke about the omnipotence of God, "What is impossible with men is possible with God" (Luke 18:27). She fixed her eye upon Jesus, and she thought, "If that is true, Christ will strengthen me." And at once she had the power to make surrender joyfully.

She wrote how, three days later, she was able to prove that surrender is an act of obedience to God's voice.

Are there any of you who have not yet found the secret of a life lived in the full joy of Jesus' countenance and love every day? Come today and claim Omnipotence to work it in you.

Let the exchange be clear. God has given you all things in Christ, all spiritual blessings, all strength, all wisdom, everything in Him. Maybe you have been holding back because you were afraid. Perhaps you have been ignorant and never understood it, but come today and say, "Absolute surrender! Lord Jesus, You shall have everything." And trust in Him, trust in His omnipotence to work in you all that God would have.

"Those who hope in the LORD will renew their strength." Count on it that as you go out today and tomorrow, not to hold fearfully to what you have got, not to try and hold onto something that was given to you, but in childlike abandonment and simple faith to say, "I am counting upon God to work it all in me."

Take that word. That is the life of strength and

of joy: "Those who hope in the LORD will renew their strength."

I have said that the first great thing we need in order to live a life of waiting upon God is to know the God upon whom we wait: study God, study to know Him.

The second is to know ourselves – to be willing and determined to accept what God reveals about us. And what does God reveal in contrast to His great omnipotence? Our utter helplessness. I said a little while ago that many people believe they have no righteousness, but they do not believe they have no strength.

Accept that word, "He gives strength to the weary and increases the power of the weak" (Isa. 40:29). What a contrast! To a person with no might, no power, God increases strength; but if a person has little power, God does not do it.

Do you not see that the great secret of waiting upon God is to be brought down to a state of utter helplessness? "I do nothing" (I cannot too often repeat these words of the blessed Son of God) "on My own" (John 8:28). What a mystery! Jesus said that – He just waited on God. And I ask you, child of God, wouldn't you like to occupy the very place that Jesus did before the Father, and in the Father's heart? Would you be willing to take that place, and to live every day as a person who has no might, is utterly helpless, and just waits upon God?

The deception is that we think we have so much strength and that we do not need to wait upon God. If a number of ships of war were sent out to sea, and were ready to start at any moment, and if the question "What are they waiting for?" were asked, the answer would likely be one of two things: either they were waiting for supplies, or waiting for orders.

Child of God, that is to be your position. First of all, you are to wait for supplies. Wait for the power of the Holy Spirit every day; wait for the strength of God every hour. Get into the habit of waiting on the Lord, and then your supplies will come.

Cultivate the habit of waiting for orders. Wait for instruction. God is willing to teach and guide His people in a way beyond their conception. Wait for instruction. Do not think, "I have my instructions in the Bible." You may mistake them or misapply them. Study and love your Bible, but remember it is God who must give the orders, and you will fail if you take them from a book. Love your Bible and fill your heart with it, but let God apply it in your daily life.

Once more, if I am to wait upon the Lord I must not only know my God and know myself, but I must study well what this word *wait* in itself implies.

It implies, first of all, patience. The Bible speaks about waiting patiently and also about waiting quietly. You must cultivate that habit. How can you do this? My answer is a very simple one.

I will put it this way. When you do morning devotions, do not, as is very often done, read the Bible and think about it and pray about it, and then get up and go. Do something else in between. Before you read, become still so that your soul may realize, "I am waiting for God to come in and take possession of me for today." That is your great need.

How many a child of God spends half an hour in his private room, in his quiet home, and he can tell you about so many beautiful thoughts in the chapter he read and what he prayed! But he has never got to the assurance where he knows, "My God is going to keep me all the day." And that is what you want to get in your morning prayer, an assurance from God that He will keep you. Then you will go out into your business in the world with His strong arm around you.

Cultivate that habit before you begin to read your Bible, and in the middle of your reading sometimes shut your eyes, just sit quiet and say, "My God, in the midst of my reading, I wait on You to make the Word living in my heart."

Then, before you pray, sit still, shut your eyes, and say, "Will God now listen to me for certain? Will I get an answer when I pray?"

Start waiting upon God, and then kneel down and pray your prayer, very shortly, perhaps, and say, "Am I waiting upon my God?" Then pray very definitely for what you want.

Let your soul grow into the blessed conscious-ness, not that you have fed on some beautiful words of God, not that you have prayed very earnestly for this and that, but let your soul go out in your quiet hour in this one consciousness, "I have been waiting upon God, and God has answered me, and God will keep me today."

Learn to come into blessed fellowship with God, and may you never, ever pray a prayer without the blessed thought, "As the eyes of slaves look to the hand of their masters, so our eyes wait upon the Lord our God." Wait quietly, wait patiently.

And then wait continually – not for one or two hours, not for one moment – but all day. Psalm 25:5 says, "My hope is in You all day long." Pray for the Holy Spirit to bring you into that blessed habit of waiting all day upon God, to give you instruction, to guide, to order, to help, to give supplies of grace and joy and strength; and God will do it. "Blessed are all who wait for Him" (Isa. 30:18).

I want to share just one more verse, "No ear has perceived, no eye has seen any God besides You, who acts on behalf of those who wait for Him" (Isa. 64:4). Learn to look to God for unexpected things. Learn to give up your thoughts about what God can do. Rest upon His promises to you, and repeat them to yourself. Then you will find that God can do far beyond what you can conceive.

Expect God, by the Holy Spirit, to work in you something completely beyond your comprehension, and God will do it – secretly, perhaps, without your feeling it – but God will do it if you trust Him for it. "Those who hope in the Lord will renew their strength."

And now, let us wait upon God, and plead with Him to make us strong in His strength, and to give us eagle wings. He has given them to us, and if we wait upon Him He will give us the grace to use them to soar "and to run and not grow weary" and to "walk and not be faint."

May God grant to us the spirit of waiting upon Him, for Jesus' sake. Amen.

Waiting on the Lord gives us

new strength for each day.